GUNS AND GUN
CONTROL
EXPOSED

GUNS AND GUN
CONTROL
EXPOSED

The Guide To

Understanding Guns

and Gun Control

D. L. Jobin

authorHOUSE®

AuthorHouse™ LLC
1663 Liberty Drive
Bloomington, IN 47403
www.authorhouse.com
Phone: 1-800-839-8640

Published by AuthorHouse 03/19/2014

ISBN: 978-1-4918-7171-3 (sc)
ISBN: 978-1-4918-7170-6 (hc)
ISBN: 978-1-4918-7169-0 (e)

Library of Congress Control Number: 2014904647

TABLE OF CONTENTS

A S A CHILD IN Canada other kids were surprised when I told them that I was a hunter and gun handler. They were always like, "Woo, you shoot **real** guns?"

As a teenager and an adult, people always asked me questions about guns, gun control and what was all the fuss about during the long gun registry debate in Canada (2006-2012). I was often the only person around them who knew anything about these topics or had any experience with firearms and could give them a straight answer. After the tragedy at Sandy Hook in the U.S. the questions all fired back up. As I was answering these questions I realized I've acquired a lot more knowledge on this subject than the standard person. And with growing up around guns and doing homework on them I've become quite knowledgeable about the history of firearms.

Eventually I decided to write this simple Guide/history book. By using history and personal experience I hope to answer the questions you have, whether they're about guns, gun control or the people behind them.

We kick-off this book with what happened to Canada's long gun registry.

For information on gun control go through Chapters 1 to 8 and 17.

To learn about where guns came from and how they came to be go through chapters 9 to 15.

To find out the relationship women have with guns go to chapter 16.

To find out what the fuss between the Anti-gun people and the Pro gun people on gun control is all about go to chapter 17.

CHAPTER 1

HOW AND WHY THE LONG GUN REGISTRY DIED

"When I say that we will crack down on crime, I don't mean that
we'll crack down on farmers or duck hunters."
—Stephen Harper

I BELIEVE THAT WHEN IT comes to public safety nothing is more dangerous than a false sense of protection.

TRAGEDY WITH GUN REGISTRATION

The sad truth is that we can not stop most killers. You don't know what someone will do when they are on drugs or pushed to their limits.

On September 13th 2006 Montreal, Quebec, Dawson College: Canada's gun control laws gave a false sense of protection to Anastasia De Sousa.

Between 12:42 pm and 1:02 pm on that horrible day, Kimveer Gill killed Anastasia, himself and injured 19 others with a Norinco HP9-1 shotgun, Beretta CX4 and a Glock pistol. Kimveer was 25 years old and all three of his guns were legally registered to his name. This was a real wake-up call on how useless gun registration really is when it comes to saving someone's life.

With Canada's strict gun laws, Kimveer probably knew that none of his victims would have the ability to fight back, making Dawson College his killing zone.

If Anastasia had a gun, giving her the ability to save herself and eliminate the threat, she might be alive today.

> "If somebody wants to kill people, they don't need a gun to do it"
>
> —Ice T

WE'RE VULNERABLE

The human body is full of vessels, arteries and vital organs. This makes us very easy to kill. Attila the Hun, Genghis Khan, Alexander the Great, William the Conqueror, Hannibal and other killers before the 13th Century had killed millions of people before the invention of firearms. History provides all the evidence that people do not need guns to kill one another.

In Canada, nobody registers their knives, ice picks or other kitchen tools.

In the wrong hands a knife can be more deadly than a gun. Knives don't jam, misfire, make a loud bang when used or run out of ammo and you don't need to be trained to know how to use them. A half inch slash wound to the side of the neck with a blade can cut the carotid artery, and the internal and external jugular veins. Once those are cut the victim has two minutes to stop the bleeding or get to the ER.

On July 30th 2008 on a Greyhound bus, Vince Li killed Tim McLean with a hunting knife. Tim was horrifically murdered and no firearm was used. Everyone on that bus was unarmed. If someone on that bus had been armed, Tim might be alive today.

Canada's gun registry did nothing to protect Anastasia De Sousa, Tim McLean and **hundreds** of other Canadians from 1995 to 2012.

The registry did tell police if there was a registered gun in a house, no doubt, but not if there's a stolen, smuggled or black market gun in the house. A black market machine gun can do a lot more damage than a registered B-B gun ever could. RCMP and city police are trained to never depend their lives on the gun registry.

The registry did not make a difference in the criminal world. Criminals don't register their guns. That's what makes them criminals and they don't care what you or I have to say to them.

> "Guns don't kill people crazy MOTHER F#%KERS kill people!"
> —Origin Unknown

The term *"Guns don't kill people. People kill people,"* is stating the fact that a gun needs a dangerous human operator to be a threat to someone. A gun is an object. It does not have a brain to have mental illness or fingers to squeeze it's own trigger. The real weapons in this world are people who are homicidal, everything else around us is a tool. As humans we are the deadliest creatures on earth.

THE MONEY

The long gun registry cost $50 for each long gun registered per year. With 30.8% of Canadians being gun owners, from 1995 to 2012, that was over $2,000,000,000 ($2 billion) total, cutting down on RCMP and city police budgets. In that time the registry did nothing to stop criminals from killing people.

On June 28th 2002 the country put Stephen Joseph Harper in office as leader of the Conservative Party. When Harper took power in 2006 he had a goal in mind to expose the long gun registry for what it was and eliminate it, but without a majority at the time there was little he could do about it, aside from fighting the Liberals with NDP leader Jack Layton backing him up.

Later in 2010 Layton betrayed Harper and the Canadian people on this issue by changing his mind and deciding to fight to change, but keep the registry. The Canadian gun owners and tax payers who hated the registry did not take this well and had enough of this harassment and endless waste of money. With Michael Ignatieff's power and Layton's betrayal, Harper was Canada's last hope to kill the Long Gun Registry. In the 2011 federal election Harper promised to get rid of the long gun registry **for good** if the voters gave him a majority.

At the end of the election Harper's Conservatives got the majority with 166 seats, Layton's NDP: 103 seats and Ignatieff's crushing defeat with only 34 seats. Michael Ignatieff stepped down and gave up leading the Liberals.

With Harper armed with the majority he needed, having Ignatieff out of Canada's House of Commons and Layton deceased, Harper got to the final vote on C-19 Long Gun Registry right after he returned from China.

Back in Canada Stephen Harper, Candice Hoeppner, the Conservatives and even two NDP members passed their vote on C-19 (getting rid of the long gun registry) and winning with 159 votes over 130 on February 22nd 2012.

On April 5th 2012 Canada's Long Gun Registry officially died and in the following November the records of the Long Gun Registry were destroyed completely. Quebec's provincial government tried to save them for themselves but, failed and now the records of the Long Gun Registry are gone.

However the Handgun Registry that started back in 1935 still lives on

CHAPTER 2

GERMANY: 1928 TO 1945

"To conquer a nation you must first disarm the citizens. Nothing drives the people harder than the sudden fear of death."

—Adolf Hitler

WITH THE GERMAN MENNONITE Resolution against slavery in 1688 I have great pride in having German ancestry from both my grandmothers. However, the first half of the 20th century in German history, is not something I'm proud of.

Back in 1918 Germany was paying the price of their defeat from World War I. The country was in high debt, causing high unemployment and almost all of the good and high paying jobs belonged to the Jewish communities, causing a lot of hatred toward Germany's Jews.

In 1928 a gun registry was passed by the German government forcing all German gun owners to have their guns registered in their names.

In 1933 a charming man named Adolf Hitler was elected Commander of the 3rd Reich and leader of Germany's Nazi Party. Hitler promised to get Germany out of it's debt problem and to provide good jobs for all the German people. But under this charm that Hitler had, was hiding a hard core racist and a real cold-blooded monster.

In 1938, Hitler used the gun registry to establish "The Nazi Weapon Act of 1938" in Germany.

1938 German Government Written Law: "A license shall not be granted if the applicant is a Jew."

The 1938 law meant all Germans who wanted to keep firearms had to register with the Nazi officials, have a background check and prove to the government that they where **Not** Jewish. Because of the registry that was passed ten years earlier the Nazis already knew which German civilians did and did not own guns.

Germany's Jews turned in their guns hoping to avoid trouble. Not everyone complied. Using the gun registry the German police, took **all** of Germany's Jew's firearms away by force and brought the people to concentration camps for resisting.

Hitler made a Germany where the only people who had guns were the police, military, Waffen-SS and Germans who were registered with the Nazi officials.

Hitler presumed that German citizens (especially Jews) were hostile and thereby exempted the Nazis from the gun control law. Hitler gave his Nazis unrestricted power to decide what kinds of guns could or could not be owned by German civilians. Germany's Jews were forbidden to own firearms, clubs or sharp-edged weapons. If any Jew was caught with a gun, club or blade he or she would be taken by police officers to a concentration camp. There they would be tortured and executed.

Led by the Waffen-SS in 1939 Hitler's Nazi war machine started invading nation after nation across Europe and was successful. The Waffen-SS were the toughest and best-trained soldiers in the world at the time. By 1941 every county in Europe besides England was crushed and under Nazi rule. Guerrilla fighters of the countries that surrendered to the Nazis fought them, but back in Germany gun control had stripped the people helpless and the Nazi police had been arresting all Jews, Gypsies, the handicapped and people that were homosexual since 1939. By that time the Nazis already had the Jews labelled with the gold star of David on the chest of their clothing and knew that they were unarmed. This made it easy for the Nazis to identify who was Jewish and take them to the concentration camps.

The Nazis, being the army and police in Germany, were armed with the best weapons in the world. The Jews having just their hands, were taken to concentration camps. In these camps they were starved, mutilated, tortured, gassed, used for experiments and executed. Think of the nastiest torture methods that were available back then, Hitler's Nazis used all of them on men, women, children and babies in these concentration camps.

Hitler's plan for world domination was going well until he made the same mistake that Napoleon Bonaparte made before him: by sending the German Army and Waffen-SS to invade Russia in 1941. The big Red Machine then set it's sights on Nazi Germany. On December 7th that same year his Japanese ally bombed a U.S. naval base in Pearl Harbor, Hawaii, awakening the wrath of the sleeping American giant. (In World War II the American's produced 100,000 tanks and other armoured vehicles, over 20,000,000 small arms and over 41,000,000,000 rounds of ammunition, enough to kill every person on the planet 17 times.)

Hitler's Italian ally dropped out in 1943, Hungarians in 1945, Romanians and Bulgarians both backed out in 1944.

On June 6th 1944 The Canadian, British and American armies stormed and took over the beaches of Normandy from the German military, marking D-Day. Hitler's clock started ticking.

By April of 1945 the Nazis were on their knees, the Red Army was in Berlin and were over-throwing them. After fighting the Canadian, British and allied armies for six long years and fighting the Russian and American armies for four years, it all became too much for even the tough Waffen-SS to handle.

With the Russian army in Berlin, Hitler knew that his final plan had failed. After he poisoned himself on April 30th 1945, he put a Walther PPK pistol to his own head and ended his life, leaving Germany and Japan to face the world alone. In the following September Japan gave up and World War II came to an end.

(The Walther PPK pistol became known as James Bond's gun as opposed to the sidearm that Adolf Hitler used to kill himself.)

Hitler did commit suicide but left his mark as one of the most famous evil men in history, the man who started the deadliest war in history, a conflict that killed as many as 78,000,000 people. **67% of them were civilians.**

Almost everyone knows who Adolf Hitler was but, what most people don't know is that he was a gun control supporter.

Before his death, Hitler used gun registration to establish gun confiscation, allowing his Nazi party to **torture and kill over 1/4 of Germany's population, over 20,000,000** innocent unarmed people, men, women, children and babies.

A lot of gun control supporters that know about this will say that what happened in Germany was a one time thing that could never happen again. That is where they are wrong. Government genocide and cold blooded murder following gun control has happened all over the world, not only in history but it's going on today.

"Those who do not remember the past are condemned to repeat it."

—George Santayana

CHAPTER 3

THE SOVIET UNION: 1917 TO 1953

"We don't let them have ideas. Why would we let them have guns?"
—Joseph Stalin

I N 1917 THE SOVIET government passed a series of laws that almost made it impossible for non-party members to own guns. They used licensing laws to tell them who did and did not have guns.

Russian government written law: "All permits for the carrying or keeping of arms are invalid and must be exchanged for new certificates," "Any violation of laws concerning rifled firearms punishable by forced labour."

At the end of the 1920's a violent man, just as evil as Hitler himself, (some say more evil then Hitler) named Joseph Stalin seized power in The Soviet Union. Thirty years of violence, torture, terror and killing was about to start.

> "If the opposition disarms, well and good. If it refuses to disarm,
> we shall disarm it ourselves."
> —Joseph Stalin

> "The only real power comes out of a long rifle."
> —Joseph Stalin

In 1927 lack of food was a problem for dictator Stalin's 5-year plan. To solve this problem he forced collectivization on the west country side. With propaganda and lies Stalin made farm life in Russia sound like paradise when it was a living hell. Starvation meant nothing to Stalin. He did not care. Prisoners were turned into slaves to be worked to death.

In 1932 Stalin cut off food supplies to entire regions killing millions by starvation. Desperate people resorted to cannibalism to avoid dying.

At the beginning of the 1930's Stalin had an absolute grip on power in Russia and for the people of the Soviet Union it became the bloodiest decade of his rule. Stalin signed thousands of death warrants to people that he accused of spying.

In 1938 Stalin saw an opportunity for world domination by letting the Germans destroy the west and he made a very big mistake by trusting and secretly signing a pact with Adolf Hitler in August of 1939. In this pact Stalin and Hitler agreed to carve up Eastern Europe.

When Hitler betrayed their pact and invaded Russia in 1941, the aggressive German Nazis got deep into Russia because of the combination of the element of surprise and because the Russian civilians were unarmed.

Even when his country was under attack, Stalin continued to terrorize his own people. He made sure that his own men were shot if they retreated from the Germans.

On the Eastern fronts of World War II the Nazi Waffen-SS did not take Russian prisoners and the Russians did not take any SS prisoners either, so this is where the fighting got very nasty.

When Stalin's Red Army finally overtook Berlin and found Hitler's body in 1945, the Russian people felt that they earned a better future but Hitler's death meant almost nothing to Stalin.

Joseph Stalin remained in power until March 1st 1953 when it was believed that he suffered a stroke, but others believed he was poisoned with a toxin used to kill rats called warfarin. He died on March 5th at age 74. He was never held accountable for his crimes of starving and working over **20,000,000** innocent people to death.

> "Injustice anywhere is a threat to justice everywhere..."
> —Dr. Martin Luther King Jr.

CHAPTER 4
CHINA: 1935 To 1952

"Political power grows out of the barrel of a gun."
—Chairman Mao Zedong

I N 1935 THE CHINESE government banned guns for civilians

1935 Chinese government written law: "Whoever, without authority or good cause is found in possession of guns for military use, shall be punished with imprisonment."

From 1942 to 1944 the Japanese Army invaded China. The Chinese Army retreated. The Chinese civilians had no firearms to fight back. They were raped, tortured, used for bayonet practice, buried alive and tied down as their own organs were cut out of them one by one. Even a visiting Nazi observer was disturbed by the torturing and killing.

1949 Chairman Mao's guerrilla communists seized power and enforced their own gun control laws.

1949 Chairman Mao's government written law: "Those who supply domestic or foreign enemies with weapons or ammunition shall be punished by death or life imprisonment." "Buying or possessing guns or ammunition for use in athletic activities or for hunting shall be punished with detention."

Chairman Mao's communists used men, women and children as tools during 38 years of madness, torturing and killing **35,000,000 to 100,000,000** unarmed innocent people.

Despite Mao's cruelty he is admired for pushing the invading Japanese army out of China during World War II and for the power that he had. The Chinese do see him as a national hero and would get offended if you reefer to him as a monster. To us it would be like someone saying that John Alexander MacDonald was a psychopath.

Chairman Mao said that, "political power grows out of the barrel of a gun." He was the one who controlled all the firearms in China.

Mao died on September 9th 1976 at age 82 from heart failure.

CHAPTER 5
Cambodia: 1956 To 1979

"Since he is of no use anymore, there is no gain if he lives and no
loss if he dies."
—Pol Pot

I 'VE NOTICED THAT MOST people in Canada have no clue who Pol Pot was but, in Cambodia almost everyone knows the dictator's name.

Back in 1956 King Sihanouk established very harsh gun laws in Cambodia.

1956 Cambodian government written law: "No one may possess more than one weapon at a time except in exceptional cases." "The permit holder may neither entrust nor loan his weapon to another person, not even family."

Pol Pot learned about Cambodia's proud past and how it's ancient civilization was ruined by invaders. This haunted Pol Pot and he wanted to regain Cambodia's proud past.

As a child Pol Pot's school was French and he was taught by Catholic nuns. The tension between Cambodian and European culture shaped Pol Pot's life. In 1949 Pol Pot was influenced by Joseph Stalin and realized that in order to escape French rule, Cambodia needed communism, and some time after 1953 Pol Pot joined the Vietnamese guerrillas just as they were on the verge of victory.

Then France agreed to give up it's colonies in southeast Asia but the Vietnamese sold Cambodia out. This betrayal caused Pol Pot to suffer from paranoia.

Pol Pot took his revolution underground and started to lead a double life.

In 1956 Pol Pot became a high school teacher but, Pol Pot's real work was in rundown safe houses. There he and his friends gathered poor people to discuss the unfairness in Cambodia's society. These communists became obsessed with secrecy and in 1962 they chose Pol Pot as their leader.

During the mid 60's in the Vietnam Civil War Pol Pot was living next to the Vietnamese border and the North Vietnamese took him under their wing. When Pol Pot returned to Cambodia he started to plan a way to restore Cambodia's greatness by eliminating all traces of the modern world. While the Americas were fighting the Viet Cong and North Vietnamese Army Pol Pot's Khmer Rouge was getting stronger by the day and by the early 70's the Khmer Rouge rebels were a deadly secretive guerrilla army. The Americans assumed that the Khmer Rouge were controlled by the Viet Cong and would ceasefire after they made peace with Vietnam in 1973.

Pol Pot secretly broke from Vietnam and insisted he would fight on.

In 1975 Pol Pot's Khmer Rouge defeated the Cambodian Army in the Civil War and seized power. Once in power, dictator Pol Pot wanted to purify Cambodia by eliminating all the religious leaders, city dwellers, Vietnamese, Chinese and other ethnic groups, all traces of capitalism and western culture including all the students, intellectuals, professionals, anyone who could speak English, French, Chinese or Vietnamese, anyone that knew anything about Cambodia's past or with a 7th grade education.

Pol Pot's Khmer Rouge didn't need any laws. Their power was the law. Cambodia's poverty level, non-violent Buddhist traditions and King Sihanouk's gun control laws, insured that very few Cambodians owned guns or were ready for any form of self defence.

Anyone who fought the Khmer Rouge and any civilians who owned guns were forced to disarm after Pol Pot became in charge.

The unarmed people were not ready for, or expecting, what the Khmer Rouge were about to do to them.

The Khmer Rouge evacuated the Cambodian cities. Thinking that this move was only temporary the Cambodian people didn't resist or take much food. The entire country was turned into a concentration camp just like Nazi Germany 36 years before.

In Pol Pot's concentration camp no one got mail, decent medical treatment or phone calls. All human relationships were shattered completely. Cambodians who were married to Vietnamese were forced to kill their spouses. Even saying a kind word to a child would cost you your life.

Kilong Ung (Cambodian Genocide survivor) said that under Pol Pot's rule, the Khmer Rouge created 150 prisons where they tortured and executed people.

People were suffocated with plastic bags, they had their toenails ripped out, they were buried alive, shot to death, beaten to death and starved to death.

In over 20,000 mass graves in Cambodia's Killing Fields the skeletons and bodies were just piled on top of each other.

This slaughter went well with Pol Pot's goal, to erase Cambodia's history and make his own history. Like Nazi Germany, Pol Pot and Khmer Rouge tortured and executed **over 1/4 of the country's population,** with over **2,000,000** dead victims in just four years. Every Cambodian family was affected and suffered losses from the Khmer Rouge's genocide.

Pol Pot's paranoia eventually caused his own undoing. In 1979, he sent the Khmer Rouge into Vietnam to kill Vietnamese civilians. The Vietnamese Army responded by attacking Cambodia. After fighting and defeating the U.S. Army Rangers, Green Berets and Navy SEALS six years earlier, it only took them one month to overthrow the Khmer Rouge and put a stop to the genocide.

Pol Pot had fled the concentration camp with some members of the Khmer Rouge. He disappeared for almost 20 years until he agreed to do an interview with American reporter Nate Thayer in 1998. In this interview he spent three hours trying to explain to Nate why he had to torture people to death and kill little babies. Pol Pot's psychological health was a disaster, not only did he deal with paranoia but, he also had DSM 4 antisocial behaviour. Meaning he could kill an innocent person, watch the life drain out of their eyes and feel no shred of remorse.

Pol Pot, Cambodia's most evil psychopath, who used gun control to torture and kill over **2,000,000** innocent unarmed people, men, women, children and babies, never apologized or faced justice for what he did. Pol Pot died two weeks after his interview with Nate, on April 15th 1998 from natural causes at age 72.

If Pol Pot didn't anger the Vietnamese, his concentration camp might have gone on until his death in 1998 or might be still killing today.

CHAPTER 6

UGANDA:
1970 TO THE PRESENT-DAY

"You cannot run faster than a bullet."
—Idi Amin

U NLIKE MANY PLACES IN Africa, Uganda used to be a nice, civil and safe place to live for the poor and middle class families. Children went to school and played in the playgrounds just like present-day Canadian children. Almost everyone smiled and said "hi" to one another, but in the 1970's, things changed.

In 1971 Idi Amin's men started killing Milton Obote's supporters and dumping them in the rivers and lakes.

On December 8th 1972 Idi Amin was elected president of Uganda and overthrew dictator Milton Obote.

Obote's government already passed laws in 1970 forbidding private citizens to own firearms. Obote was hated very much. The Ugandans were sure that Idi Amin would be better because Amin was described as a clown, a funny friendly man and a gentle giant but, Amin was much worse than Obote and a very violent man.

Idi Amin immediately ordered to kill all the soldiers that he thought had poor loyalty, over **60,000** men. Several months later Amin claimed that God had ordered him to throw every Asian out of Uganda and then the English people. Amin commandeered their businesses and land and gave it to his crowns. After that, Uganda turned to chaos.

In order to make sure no one resisted, Amin made it illegal for 3 or more people to be together if one had a gun.

Like Joseph Stalin, Adolf Hitler, Chairman Mao and Pol Pot, Idi Amin did not want his victims to fight back. Firearms were seized by him. Amin's personal agents started to torture and mutilate rival tribes, people and anyone Amin disliked.

These victims were laid down in gutters so the blood would be easy to wash off.

Most of the Ugandans had no guns to resist Amin's cruelty. This madness went on for 8 years.

In order to distract the people from his carnage he sent his army to invade Tanzania in 1978. The highly armed and trained Tanzanian Army easily defeated Amin's men who were used to killing civilians unarmed by Obote and Amin's gun control laws. The Tanzanians did not believe Amin's withdrawal and invaded Uganda. They took Kampala in 1979 and in Amin's villa they found the photos of his tortured victims, but Amin already left Uganda.

During his rule Idi Amin mutilated his ministers and one of his four wives in 1975 and kept their heads in his fridge as a warning to others. Amin also kept pictures of the people his men tortured and killed for his own sick twisted pleasure.

Uganda's rivers were choking with Amin's dead victims.

In 1979 Amin was overthrown and he moved to Saudi Arabia. He lived there in peace for the following 24 years until he died on August 16th 2003 from kidney failure at age 75.

This happy guy who used gun control to **torture and kill over 300,000** innocent unarmed people never faced justice or prosecution.

In Kevin Macdonald's 2006 film "The Last King of Scotland" starring Forest Whitaker, shows what kind of a man Idi Amin was and how he hid his evil side.

Idi Amin may have left Uganda and died but, since 1986 the Lord's Resistance Army led by Joseph Kony continues to use gun control to terrorize Uganda today. The LRA know that the Ugandan parents are still unarmed from Obote's and Amin's gun control laws and are helpless to save their children from them or resist Kony's power.

Kony mutilates their faces to strike fear into anyone who stands up against him. Using gun control he and his LRA have kidnapped and raped over 40,000 children. The LRA forces these kids to kill their own parents, then sells the little girls as prostitutes and uses the boys as soldiers in the Lord's Resistance Army by giving them black market weapons. Kony and his LRA have already murdered over **400,000** innocent people. From 2008 to 2012 alone the LRA have killed over **2,400** innocent unarmed people.

Today the LRA's power is still fuelled by having black market weapons and the gun control law that makes it illegal for any civilians to fight back.

Most of The Lord's Resistance Army fighters are 7 to 15 years old.

CHAPTER 7

UNITED STATES: 1619 TO THE PRESENT-DAY

"To disarm the people . . . is the most effective way to enslave them."
—George Mason

T HE SECOND AMENDMENT RIGHT to The Constitution of The United States of America is: "A well regulated Militia, being necessary to the security of a free State, the right of the people to keep and bear Arms, shall not be infringed."

Anyone today who has been to the United States will say it is a good country with it's freedom and it's friendly American people, but the U.S. has an ugly past and racist gun control laws in its history.

Back in 1619 the Americans started using slavery, and slaves had no rights at all so the 2nd Amendment to The Constitution did not apply to them. Slavery went on until 1865. Thousands of Africans were kidnapped, brought to the States, whipped, beaten and forced to work hard without pay. As horrible as this was, this is what made the United States the world's richest county.

1806 Louisiana written law: "No slave may use firearms even in self-defence. He may hunt with firearms only with his master's written permission."

1825 Florida written law: White citizen patrols "shall enter into all Black houses and lawfully seize arms, weapons and ammunition."

1866 Alabama, 1831 Florida, post-Civil War Louisiana and 1852 Mississippi written law: "Free Blacks may not carry firearms."

1866 Alabama written law: "It shall not be lawful for any freed man, mulatto, or free person of color to own firearms or other deadly weapons."

1906 Mississippi written law: "Dealers must record the race of all buyers of pistols and ammunition."

If a slave had enough courage and luck in the 1840's, 50's and 60's he or she could escape their plantation, hide in a wagon or walk the Underground Railroad into Canada, where not only slavery was made illegal in the mid 1700's but, where they would be legal equals to whites.

(From 1850 to 1865 over 20,000 slaves escaped slavery through the Underground Railroad and resettled in Ontario, Quebec, New Brunswick and Nova Scotia. Although there was still racism in Canada, they were able to get paying jobs, their own land, the right to vote and the right to have a gun. Canada had civil rights past over 120 years before America did. Slave-catchers who had tracked and recaptured escaped slaves in the northern states, learned very quickly **not** to attempt this north of the border. Not only did some of the former slaves have guns but, if you were caught taking people against their will, black or white, in 1800's Canada, the Canadian authorities hanged prisoners who were caught kidnapping people. Whether any Confederates attempted this is lost to history.)

In 1861 Abraham Lincoln had enough of the south and a war broke out to end slavery nation wide. After four years of civil war bloodshed the Confederates surrendered to the Union ending slavery in America but that still did not mean equal rights for African Americans. Several weeks before the south surrendered in 1865, Abraham Lincoln was shot in the head and killed. Andrew Johnson was then put in charge and he shared the fear that the white south had on the possibility of an uprising of the former slaves. Because of this political fear and the influence that the Ku Klux Klan or KKK had at the time, one of America's first federal gun laws was to make it illegal for a non-white to own a gun in the 1870's.

With the African Americans unarmed, the Ku Klux Klan started beating up and killing African Americans by shooting or hanging them. **Tens of Thousands** of unarmed innocent African Americans were murdered by the racists. This went on until December 1ˢᵗ 1955, when in Montgomery, Alabama an African American woman named Rosa Parks took a stand by sitting down, as strange as that might sound. By refusing to give up her seat on a bus to a white man, in the U.S. she was breaking the law at the time and was arrested. Rosa's actions that day stirred up a hornets nest across the United States. Rosa Parks, Martin Luther King Jr., Charlton Heston, Malcolm X, W. E. B. Du Bois and the other Civil rights activists all fought the United States government for the equal rights for African Americans and in 1968 they finally won, or so they thought.

> "The Gun Control Act of 1968 was passed not to control guns but to control blacks."
> —Robert Sherrill, journalist and supporter of gun control.

(Before civil rights were passed, Martin Luther King was denied a gun permit, even though he was receiving death threats on a daily basis from the KKK and his house was fire bombed.

Martin Luther King, a Christian minister was **denied self defence** in the United States because of his skin colour. Nevertheless he still fought for equal rights and for a stop to racism. On April 4ᵗʰ 1968 the law still had him unarmed and helpless. As he was at the Lorraine Motel in Memphis, Tennessee, he was shot in the neck and murdered.)

The Million Mom March and other American gun control activists want to disarm the American civilians just like they did to the African Americans back in the 1870's. Even though Rosie O'Donnell wants to deny Americans the right of self-defence, she has an armed bodyguard for the protection of herself and her children.

Post 1968's gun laws in the United States might target criminals but, the innocent law-abiding Americans are the ones who pay the painful price.

On October 16th 1991 in Killeen, Texas, a young doctor named Suzanna Gratia was having lunch with her parents at a Luby's cafeteria. Suzanna usually carries a handgun (a .38 revolver) in her purse for self-defence but, the law at the time made Suzanna leave her sidearm in her car in the parking lot. At 12:35 pm a truck crashed through the window and a madman named George Hennard got out holding two semi-automatic handguns. He then started shooting the customers to death. Suzanna identified the immediate threat, made sure that George was clear of innocent bystanders, became sure of her target and beyond and reached into her purse. Then she's reminded that self-defence is locked up in the parking lot. Her father tried to rush George but was gunned down. Suzanna's mother ran over to, and cradled her dying husband. All Suzanna did and could have done, was watch in horror, run out a broken window, look back and see George shoot her mother in the head at point blank range. Twenty three innocent people died in that tragedy and the law that made Suzanna defenceless was why most of them did.

Today Suzanna fights against the people who try to enforce the gun free zones that killed her parents, Anastasia De Sousa, the 12 dead from Aurora's movie theatre, the children of Sandy Hook, the victims of Virginia Tech and Columbine.

In the air it is illegal for passengers to carry a gun on planes, not just over U.S. ground but globally too. On September 11th 2001 at 8:46 am, over New York, New York, 19 hijacking terrorists used that law and box cutters to take over two planes and destroy the two World Trade Centre buildings, killing nearly **3,000** people, injuring over 6,000 others, scaring not only the entire country but, the whole world that horrible day.

(After the 9/11 attacks in New York, New York, gun sales went up in the U.S. by 70% and ammunition went up 140%.)

On July 20th, 2012 in the Century movie theatre (a gun-free zone) on 14300 E. Alameda Avenue, in Aurora, Colorado, James Holmes entered the theatre, setting off tear gas and started shooting off rounds into the unarmed audience with a Remington 870 shotgun, two Glock model 22's and a S&W M&P15 rifle (a very similar gun to the widely used AR-15).

James killed 12 people and injured 62 others. Eight more people were hurt trying to escape before the police got James under control.

There were several other movie theatres closer to James's home. The difference between the theatre he went to and the others, is that the one he went to was a gun-free zone. The ones closer to his home allowed the movie goers to carry their guns if they had a right to carry permit. James knew that he would be the one who was safe in a gun-free zone. If he went into a place where he did not know who was armed and who was not he himself would possibly have been dead before he fired the fourth shot.

They say gun-free zones keep people safe but, the reality side of that is that without security and metal detectors, they have the reverse effect. That day the gun free zone that was in that theatre cost 12 innocent people their lives.

AMERICAN SCHOOL NIGHTMARES

> "If it's crazy to call for putting police and armed security in our
> school to protect our children, then call me crazy."
> —Wayne LaPierre

In the 1990's in the state of Colorado it was illegal for a teacher to bring their gun(s) to work.

On April 20th 1999 in Jefferson County, the teachers of Columbine High School obeyed the law and all went to work unarmed. Two teenage murderers, Eric David Harris and gun control supporter Dylan Bennet Klebold armed with a TEC-DC9, Hi-Point 995 Carbine, Savage 67H pump-action shotgun, Stevens 311D double barrelled sawed-off shotgun, 99 explosives and 4 knives entered the school and started shooting people. The students and unarmed teachers who had no ways of protecting themselves, could only do what they could by trying to escape. Before Eric and Dylan committed suicide, they killed 12 students, one teacher and injured 21 others.

Just like 1999 Colorado, in 2007 in Virginia it was illegal for teachers to be armed on school grounds. On April 16th 2007, in the Virginia Tech school in the town of Blacksburg, the teachers all arrived unarmed. Seung-Hui Cho, who was inspired by Eric Harris and Dylan Klebold, armed himself with two semi-automatic handguns, (a Glock 19 and a Walther P22.) Seung-Hui Cho then entered the school and killed 32 people and injured 23 before turning one of his handguns on himself.

In Connecticut, it is illegal for a teacher to carry his or her gun at work. In Newtown on December 14th 2012 the teachers of Sandy Hook Elementary School all followed the law. After killing his mother that morning, Adam Lanza, armed with two handguns and a rifle (a Glock, a SIG Bauer and a semi-automatic AR-15,) entered the school, killing the principal, the school psychologist, 3 teachers and 20 children most of them only 6 years old. Unable to defend themselves, the helpless kids and unarmed teachers could only try to hide until the NPD (Newtown Police Department) arrived, **by which time** Adam Lanza had already taken his own life.

This tragedy really hit home for me not just because I was an uncle of three at the time but, because three of the children's names were Dylan, Emilie and Benjamin and the psycho's name was Adam. My name is Dyllon, I have a cousin named Adam, I have a niece and a nephew named Emily and Benjamin.

Clark Aposhian, Chairman from Utah Shooting Sports Council, had over 200 teachers come to get the training and the carry permits to make sure that what happened in Connecticut could not happen in their schools.

HOW YOUR GUNS KEEP YOU ALIVE

In Maryland, West Taylor was attacked when he answered his own front door, by two intruders with a baseball bat. West had his Walther PPK at the time of the attack. He fell back in his house and fired several shots at his attackers. Both of them started to run, one fell down in the yard. West told his wife to call 911 and an ambulance. With his Walther empty West dropped it on his stairs and got to his 9mm Glock that had a 10-round magazine in the closet and walked to the man who tried to kill him. At that moment the man's accomplices tried to back West over with a car. West pointed his Glock at the car, shot several rounds and the car drove away. The second suspect was caught by police. It turned out she was a woman and she was sentenced to four years in jail.

The man who tried to kill and rob West had a criminal record of second-degree assault, fourth-degree burglary and had spent 6 months in prison.

(Like Canada, in the state of Maryland it is illegal for a law-abiding person to have over a 10-round magazine in their handgun. It took more than 10 rounds for West to save himself and his wife. He was lucky he had two handguns. West is a retired policeman from Washington D.C. and in his 42 years with a police force he never took a gun from a criminal, where the criminal got it legally.)

Ridiculous Law Ideas

"Limiting the law-abiding's ability to defend innocent life, is
NOT the answer to crime!"
—D.L. Jobin

In 2009 Barack Obama was elected president of the United States. The Americans embraced him because Gorge W. Bush had became unpopular since 9/11 and the Americans were sure that Obama would be better. Back on September 9th 2008 Obama <u>claimed he believed in America's 2nd Amendment</u> and said he **would not take away** anyone's rifle, shotgun, handgun or any of Americans guns. After his operation "Fast and Furious" (running illegal guns to the Mexican Drug Cartel that killed American Border Patrol Agent Brian Terry) and the Sandy Hook tragedy, he betrayed the law-abiding American gun owners. In the months following Sandy Hook, Obama tried to use the tragedy and operation Fast and Furious to try enforce gun control, little by little, starting with a ban on firearms that have over a 10-round capacity.

Anti-gun people say that, "10-round magazines instead of 30-round magazines would cut down on the number of fatalities." (In that case they should ban knives. Knives have infinite magazines, no reloading.)

I got someone to put a clock on me while I reloaded a box magazine-fed rifle with dummy ammunition. As it turns out, taking an empty magazine out of it's rifle, taking a full one out of my pocket, putting the full one in the rifle and then chambering a round only takes 2-3 seconds; the odd time 4 seconds. With a little bit of practise with a handgun; 1.3 seconds and I'm just your average hunter, you do not need to be a magician to get this kind of speed. (I know of a man named Jerry Miculek, with a 6-shot swing out **revolver** get 12 shots off in 2.99 seconds including reload time.) It can be done in 4-5 seconds with almost no experience. To a monster that has unarmed targets trapped in a classroom-sized environment and the police as far as 30 minutes away, 2-3 seconds, 1.3 seconds or even 4-5 seconds is all the time in the world with fish in a barrel. Sad but true.

To think that a 10-round capacity limit law would have saved any children at Sandy Hook is not only crazy but, to try to enforce it is a dangerous thing to do. I have been operating pellet guns since I was four years old and 22. rifles since I was five. One of the things that I can tell you that a person who's never even touched a gun could, is that a firearm with a smaller magazine has a tendency to force it's user to pick their shots more carefully on multiple targets. If Adam had 10-round magazines he may have killed more children in a very similar period of time.

Also, if a teacher who is trying to save their own life and the lives of their students has only 10 rounds to deal with an immediate threat, and the perpetrator, who is not afraid to die, has 30 rounds to deal with the teacher, the law would be in favour of the perpetrator.

It has been proven by Cody R Wilson that with a 3D Printer you can build a functional 30-round detachable magazine out of plastic to fit into a gun that takes detachable magazines. And it is not rocket science at all. It can easily be done.

On April 17ᵗʰ 2013 Obama's attempt for the 10-round capacity limit law in America failed. (Americas violent crime rate has been dropping since 1992.)

Obama said that the gun laws he's trying to enforce are to make the children safer. For every child in America who dies from a gunshot injury, 4 of them die in swimming pools and 14 are killed by traffic.

FEAR

In December of 2012 alone there were 2,780,000 background checks in the United States. That's 39% higher than what they were in November of 2012.

In the following month after the tragedy at Sandy Hook, there were approximately 250,000 new NRA (National Rifle Association) members and there were over 4,700,000 guns sold in the United States (most of them AR-15s and semi-autos with over 10-round magazines). By May of 2013 the NRA had 600,000 new members.

Throughout the months following Sandy Hook the American gun stores could not keep up with their new and old customers who were buying everything off the shelves. For a period of time in Chicago, Illinois you could not buy a gun. Every single store in the city was sold out completely. With the fear that the AR-15 would become illegal very soon the Americans who always thought of getting an AR were buying them. This fear brought up new buyers for not only AR-15s but any semi-auto gun with a larger than a 10-round magazine. The gun companies that make the AR-15 and AR-15 like rifles, like Bushmaster and ArmaLite, could not keep up with the demand for them. (They tried to slow down the demand by charging more for them, from around $800 U.S. up to $2,000 U.S.) Moving America's gun ownership from 88.8% to 89%. There is now more firepower in the hands of American civilians than in the hands of the entire Chinese and Indian armies combined.

Some people argue that America's 2nd Amendment refers to flintlock muzzleloaders only, (guns that needed to have black powder poured down their barrel, then ram a bullet down, pour more powder in a flash pan and cock the hammer all for one shot) not military style firearms. In the present-day that is a fair argument but what these people seem to forget is that flintlock muzzleloaders were military firearms.

If you are an American, remember that your 2nd Amendment is the right that allows rights to exist and if you give in a centimetre you will lose the whole kilometre. The NRA is the strongest, if not the only wall protecting your rights.

As a law-abiding Canadian, I can tell you that living in a country with a Federal gun registry and a 5-round magazine capacity limit law on semi-autos is not only scary but a real pain in the A$$!

> "The right of the people to keep and bear arms shall not be infringed; a well armed and well regulated militia being the best security of a free country..."
> —James Madison

CHAPTER 8

CANADA:
1935 TO THE PRESENT-DAY

"When you harass a harmless law-abiding gun owner like myself and
ignore the guys with criminal records who can buy whatever weapon
they want off the black market, that's how violent crime goes up."
—D.L. Jobin

L ET'S HAVE A LOOK at gun control and government in Canada and our own history, eh? When the Europeans came to Canada in the early 1600's they brought the matchlock musket along.

In the battle between the natives and the white man, the flintlock and blasting cap muzzleloader went head to head with the bow and arrow and emerged on the winning side. The gun became a part of our heritage. It was the difference between food on the table or not. If you are attacked it could be the difference between life and death.

During Saskatchewan's prohibition of alcohol (1917-1925), Italian American Al Capone, who was wanted for bootlegging & murder in the United States, allegedly moved into the tunnels of Moose Jaw to make and sell booze illegally. When Al Capone came to Canada his Thompson submachine gun came with him.

The Thompson submachine gun (also known as the Chicago typewriter) can fire 600 to 1,000 rounds a minute. Eventually Capon left the tunnels and went back to the U.S.

After seeing the devastation of the Thompson's firepower it became illegal for civilians to own fully-automatic firearms (machine guns) in this country in 1935. Registration on handguns became mandatory and it still is today.

On December 6th 1989 at École Polytechnique. Marc Lépine, armed with a Mini-14 rifle and a hunting knife, shot 28 people killing fourteen women, injuring ten other women and four men in under twenty minutes before turning his rifle on himself.

In 1995 the Liberals, led by Prime Minister Jean Chrétien, did not blame Marc Lépine for the tragedy or go after Canada's psychopaths. They blamed the gun and it's large ammunition capacity, so by standing on the graves of these women, they came after the law-abiding and ignored the criminals. They came after the magazines and passed Bill C-68, or the Firearms Act, ushering in stricter gun control regulations, forcing all law-abiding Canadian gun owners to register their long rifles and shotguns. Long barrelled semi-auto shotguns and large calibre semi-auto rifles could no longer have a 6 or more round magazine capacity. This caused a lot of legitimate collectors and hunters to give everything up or move to the United States.

There are some guns in Canada that are Restricted or illegal because of how they look. Really? In this case we should ban facial and body piercings because they look awful.

During the worst flood in Alberta history in 2013 the RCMP used the PAL system to seize the guns from the people of the town of High River by forcing their way into evacuated homes. Called "Gun Grab at High River", it is one of the biggest human violations in Canadian history. I do not hold this against all members of the RCMP. I do consider them as an ally but what happened in High River, Alberta did not have to happen.

On March 3rd 2005 just outside Mayerthorpe, Alberta, a man named James Roszko, who had a history of violent and sexual offences, opened fired on six RCMP Officers, killing officers Peter Schiemann, Lionide Johnston, Brock Myrol, Anthony Gordon and himself in his quonset shed with a H&K G3. The other two officers survived the shooting and were not injured.

When you ask: how could this have happened in Canada? I will answer it with the truth and put it out in the open. Here it is:

<u>Canada has one of the worst justice systems in the world.</u> (A prisoner in Saskatchewan, who is serving a life sentence for killing a woman by locking her in a closet and setting fire to the house, is using taxpayer's dollars to sue for being treated poorly in prison. Seriously!?)

When it comes to Canadian jails we're too soft on the criminals. Prisoners here are treated like hotel guests who are not allowed to leave. We could learn a thing or two from Russia and Mexico when it comes to prisons. With no death penalty (even though the majority of law-abiding Canadians and RCMP's want the death penalty back) and overflowing prisons, we have no choice but to release violent people like James Roszko.

Roszko only spent roughly a total of two years in jail for assault and rape, because until the tragedy, he never murdered anyone and Canada's justice systems kept letting him out, until four RCMP officers went in his quonset shed alive and came out in body bags!

The H&K G3 that James used is a 20-round battle rifle that can switch to fully-automatic and it's heavy 7.62×51 mm or 308 bullets can easily punch through your standard Kevlar armour that is made to stop pistol bullets. The G3 is illegal for civilian use in Canada due to it's 20-round magazine and its ability to go on fully-automatic. At the time of the tragedy James Roszko's police record prohibited him from owning a legal firearm. This might make you ask the question: how does a man with a criminal record as long as James's get a fully-automatic battle rifle in Canada, a country with harsh gun laws and a long gun registry at the time? The answer is simple: **JAMES ROSZKO WAS A CRIMINAL, HE GOT IT BY BREAKING THE LAW!**

(Criminals don't register their guns. They get them illegally so if they lose it at a crime scene it can't be traced back to them.)

James Roszko either traded cannabis (marijuana) over the U.S. border for it, or bought it off the black market.

> "I am like any other man. All I do is supply a demand."
> —Al Capone

Smuggled and black market guns over the U.S. border is big business. It is the largest illegal trade over the border. It is mostly about <u>Canadian drugs for American guns</u>. Every year, it is estimated by ATF that **tens of thousands** of firearms (mostly handguns) are smuggled over and under the American border in an exchange for drugs or to be sold illegally to Canadian criminals and gangs.

(There is around 6,415 km of U.S. border to the south, plus another 2,475 km with Alaska.)

Border Patrol can not do a strip-search on every single vehicle that comes over the American border. An illegal gunrunner can get a handgun in America for $300 (or if the handgun is tied to a murder, as low as $75 of the street), blend in with the tourists at the border, smuggle it into Canada and resell it on the streets of Toronto or Vancouver to someone with a criminal record for a price up to $3,000. Depending on what the dollar is that's around <u>$2,700 to $2,925 profit for just one handgun.</u> It is supply and demand and has been going on since the 1930's. It shows no sign of stopping or slowing down.

(I do **NOT** blame America or it's 2ⁿᵈ Amendment for illegal gunrunning and we should not blame America for the problems that our government lets happen.)

Canada and the United States are the worlds two biggest trading partners. Our neighbour to the south **is** also the second largest arm supplier in the world, only rivalled by Russia.

We are located between Russia and the United States, the top two biggest gun exporters in the world, both legal and illegal. As long as we have gangs and drug dealers in Canada there will always be smuggled and black market weapons in Canada. You can pass all the laws you want, harassing the law-abiding people of Canada it is just going to make it easier for the criminals, that always say, "F#%K the law, I can just get a gun of the street. I got a source." If the bad guy has money he will always gets his gun of choice.

Al Capone might be gone, but other gangs still blood bathe the streets of Canada over drugs and blood money. When you have gangs and drugs in the same place at the same time, you're going to have smuggled, stolen and black market guns in the wrong hands.

When someone break and enters your home in most states in the U.S. the law says that you can shoot them.

Here in Canada the government lets dangerous criminals, rapists and murderers out of prison all the time, because they feel sorry for them, maybe they had a bad childhood. Polar bear $#%T! You are always responsible of your own actions!

Self-defence is practically illegal for the law-abiding in this country. The law says that you have to have your guns locked up separate from ammo. If a criminal breaks in your house to harm you or your kids, and you kill him to save yourself or your children, you will be facing murder charges.

(Vince Li, who killed Tim McLean on a Greyhound bus by cutting his head off with a knife back in 2008 is being released.)

Gun control laws have never been an inconvenience to Canadian gangs and murderers. Most of them laugh because the government will just let them out of jail sooner or later so they can keep preying on innocent people. In point of fact they love the idea of gun control disarming their victims in this place we call a free country.

As you're reading this very book there are hundreds of illegal guns being smuggled into Canada in an exchange for drugs and/or to be sold illegally to criminals and not only over and under the American border but, from overseas as well.

THE NUMBER ONE REASON WHY GENOCIDES AND
ILLEGAL GUNRUNNERS ARE THRIVING AROUND
THE WORLD IS BECAUSE OF GUN CONTROL.

The Globe's Top Three Firearm Suppliers Are:
Russia, The United States and China

CHAPTER 9

WHERE THE GUN CAME FROM

"I made it to protect the motherland."
—Mikhail Kalashnikov

BEFORE THE FIRST CANNON was invented in the 1200's AD the Chinese had already been using gunpowder for around 200 years in their fireworks. They eventually discovered that if you seal one end of a pipe, poured gunpowder, then a lead ball down the other end and ignited the powder, the explosion inside the barrel would fire the ball out at a very high speed, faster than any arrow.

The original cannon had 8 wheels and it needed 2 oxen to pull it.

In the 14th century people started building smaller cannons that an individual could carry and operate. These were called hand cannons.

The hand cannon made armour useless and made the knight disappear.

How they worked was you'd put a powder and ball in the barrel and put more powder in the touch-hole and ignite it with a flame. This was very difficult to do in the heat of battle but, at the time it was the only way to defeat a knight in shining armour.

In 1475 the matchlock musket was invented. This meant to fire the gun you didn't have to ignite the powder by hand, what you did was light the wick, open the flash pan, squeeze the trigger that pulls the arm that held the lit wick into the flash pan. This would light the powder and fire the gun. The matchlock musket is what kept the explorers alive.

In early 16th century Hernán Cortés used his harquebus matchlock to defeat the Aztecs. At the beginning of the 1600's it first came to North America with the Europeans in Newfoundland.

In the mid 17th century, the flintlock started to replace the matchlock.

The wheel lock was also something new but, it was expensive to build and was less reliable than the flintlock and didn't became very popular.

In the 1700's some flintlocks started to have grooves that twisted in the barrel. This meant that the bullet would spin in flight making it fly straighter. This is called rifling. However this made reloading take twice as long and the rifle was originally used for hunting not combat.

According to Paul Suda (18th Century Weapons Expert), in the U.S.A.'s Revolutionary War General George Washington had his men use both the flintlock musket (Brown Bess) and flintlock rifle (Pennsylvania Long Rifle). The muskets had faster reload times. The rifles had greater range. This is called hybrid warfare. With hybrid warfare General George Washington was able to lead his men to victory over the most powerful army in the world at the time (the British) and these guns were a big factor.

CHAPTER 10
THE SHOTGUN

"The clash-clash from a shotgun is the universal sound for, get the
F#%K out of my house!"
—Most owners of pump action shotguns

I DON'T KNOW ABOUT YOU but, if I was a criminal who just broke into someone's house in the dark, I would really rather hear a dog than hear the clash-clash from a pump action shotgun, because the loud BANG that followed it was the last sound a lot of criminals heard.

In the 1400's lots of cannons were being loaded with small lead balls that spread out. This was called grapeshot.

Phillipe Simon (Napoleonic Historian) said that Napoleon Bonaparte himself used grapeshot in his cannons.

During that time French bird hunters discovered that this concept worked in hand-held muskets. Shooting a bird in flight was no longer dependant on luck.

The shotgun's original purpose was for hunting birds but they became extremely effective in a fight. The blunderbuss was specifically invented for war and self-defence.

Back in the old days you had to hunt for your food and you could only afford one gun. Most of the time it would be a shotgun because of how versatile it is. With a double barrel shotgun you could have one barrel loaded with pellets called shot for birds and the other loaded with buckshot (single bullet) for big game.

Soldiers, police and gangsters all loved the shotgun because by shooting a group of pellets you had a better chance of hitting your target. They were more effective than handguns. Multiple pellets flying into the body had a much better chance of causing death as opposed to a single pistol bullet.

On the covered wagons of the old west the passenger in the front would have a shotgun to stop trouble if you came across it. Today people still call "shotgun" when they want to sit in the front seat of a vehicle.

The most common shotgun today is probably the Remington 870, a pump action gun that has an 18 to 30 inch barrel. Bird hunters, the Canadian Forces, the RCMP and city police all across Canada and the world use the Remington 870. Almost all American police except the police in Los Angeles use the Remington 870. The Los Angeles Police Department replaced their Remington 870s with an Italian shotgun made by Benelli. The Benelli M4 is a semi-automatic shotgun designed in 1998 and it is a fabulous shotgun.

Despite being in the truck in every RCMP cruiser and in almost every police and military vehicle in the world, the shotgun still is what it's always has been, a tool for hunting birds.

CHAPTER 11

THE 1ST GUNS THAT CAN BE FIRED OVER AND OVER

"It always seems impossible until its done."
—Nelson Mandela

MUZZLELOADERS NEED TO BE loaded from the front: powder, then ram the ball, then put a percussion cap on, all just for just one shot. Someone could get 3 or 4 shots off a minute if he or she was lucky.

Back then everybody's dream was to have something that could be fired again and again without reloading. In 1836 Samuel Colt made this dream a reality by inventing the revolver.

When Samuel Colt was a teenager working on a ship he saw the way the ship was steered. He's watched the way the wheel spun and locked into place. He wondered, could this concept be used to make a gun with multiple chambers that could fire again and again? The answer was yes. (The chamber is the part of the gun behind the barrel where the bullet sits before it's fired)

For the first time in history you had a wheel inside a gun with six rotating chambers allowing you to shoot six times without reloading. This technology at the time was amazing and it made Colt's name. When America's Civil War broke out in 1861, Samuel Colt only manufactured it for the North. It was so advanced that the Confederates had to copy it in order to compete, but they were inferior because the Confederate ones were made of brass as opposed to iron. Before Samuel's gun achieved victory for the North, he died in 1862 at the age of 47. Colt's widow took over running his plant and even after it burned down she had it rebuilt.

In 1861 Christopher Spencer came up with a different workable design, a rifle that could carry 7 rounds and handle the battlefield. It was a big advantage over the muzzleloader.

In the 1850's Ben Henry invented the lever action rifle and in 1862 it went up for sale but, the American Civil War was almost over by the time it went into service. The Confederates that were unfortunate enough to come across it said, "That damn Yankee gun. They'd load it on Sunday and shoot at us all week."

Once rifles started to use actual shells with bullet, primer and casing all in one called a self contained cartridge, people wanted the same for their handguns.

The Colt company came up with the Colt single action army.

Two other well known gun making partners named Horace Smith and Daniel B. Wesson also took the revolver to the next step. They came up with revolvers that took smokeless powder and even could be reloaded on the back of a galloping horse which in the wild west was important.

Smith & Wesson revolvers have almost been in every military and police force in the world at one time or another. (Even today the RCMP use the Smith & Wesson semi-automatic 5946)

In 1935 Smith & Wesson introduced the .357 Magnum that the police wanted to use to penetrate armed bodies and bullet proof glass of gangster cars.

In 1955 Smith & Wesson came up with another Magnum that eventually became the most famous hand gun in the world. The Smith & Wesson model 29 in .44 Magnum was the most powerful hand gun in the world at the time until 2003 when Smith & Wesson came up with the 500 S&W Magnum. After Clint Eastwood carried the model 29 in the film "Dirty Harry" that came out in 1971, the Smith & Wesson company could not keep up with the orders that were coming in for their model 29 in the .44 Magnum.

There is an old saying that "God made man and woman. Samuel Colt made them even."

The revolver was also called "the peace maker, the gun that tamed the wild west, the equalizer and the smoke wagon."

Billy the Kid carried a Colt Lightning revolver. The Jesse James gang depended their lives on their peacemakers.

In the American wild west almost everyone carried a revolver on their hip.

Even long after semi-automatic pistols were invented in the late 1800's, police still used revolvers until the beginning of the 1990's. Colt, S&W and other manufacturers still make and sell revolvers today. There are collectors and shooters in the 21st century that still love them. I like revolvers myself and Smith & Wesson make my favourite ones. I'm not saying that there's anything wrong with other companies, just that when it comes to revolvers I just happen to be a Smith & Wesson guy.

Americans still use revolvers for self defence. They are more accurate and reliable than semi-automatic pistols. That said, they do have their limits with the 4 to 10 rounds that can be chambered in these guns.

John Moses Browning was a 10-year old kid when he built his first rifle.

When he was 23 he came across a gun so poorly made he laughed at it. His father agreed that it was not a good design. John Browning knew he could build a better gun and he did. He came up with a single shot design that was very strong and well made. Shortly after his single shot design got out the Winchester company bought the design from John Browning for $8,000. Browning's single shot became the Winchester 1885, the most widely used single shot rifle of the era.

From that moment on John Browning was able to spend enough time to design even more guns. Browning's next amazing design was the Winchester 1886

Winchester paid $50,000 for this design, but the gun was worth it. The Winchester 1886 was a fantastic gun but it did have a problem. It was heavy and cowboys wanted a lighter gun, so John Browning designed a lighter version of it, the 1892. Winchester could not wait to get it. Just like Colt's revolver every cowboy had one and it took the same ammo, the 44-40.

Over the next 2 years Winchester bought 11 more of Browning's designs. One was the model 1894. It became the most popular lever action around.

Mexico's Robin Hood, Pancho Villa and his bandits used the 1894, loved it and the 1895, also designed by Browning.

John Browning's next gun was the Winchester 1897 the first widely successful pump action shotgun. That was manufactured until 1957.

In Europe the lever action was unpopular because in 1824 a German man named Johann Nicolaus von Dreyse invented the bolt-action rifle. A rumour that still goes on today is that he got the idea from looking at a door bolt.

The bolt-action rifle's mechanical action gave it a slower rate of fire than the lever action, but it was preferred over the lever action due to its superior range, accuracy and reliability.

The bolt-action rifle was issued as the standard small arm for almost every army and it saw combat in dozens of wars including World War I and World War II. By the 1960's they were replaced with semi and fully automatic rifles for the standard small arm. Despite being replaced the bolt-action is still being used today by military and police snipers, hunters and competition shooters.

CHAPTER 12
THE SNIPER RIFLE

"One shot, one kill"
—Sniper's motto

I N THE AMERICAN CIVIL War some of the northern fighters put telescopes with cross-hairs on their blasting cap muzzleloaders. This gave them the ability to identify high ranking Confederate officers and taking them out at a much farther distance than with iron sights.

Since the American Civil War the use of the sniper rifle has spread across the world and it's used by every army and police SWAT department.

On November 22nd 1963, the 35th President of the United States, John F. Kennedy was claimed to have been assassinated by Lee Harvey Oswald with a sniper rifle in Dallas, Texas.

The worlds farthest kill shot by a sniper was done by a Canadian sniper named Robert Furlong in Afghanistan, hitting a Taliban fighter at 2.4 kilometres away with a .50 Cal BMG McMillan Tac-50.

At 2.4 kilometres that .50 Cal bullet is flying for four seconds. That's a lot of time for the wind to change but, Robert Furlong and his spatter were able to pull it off, breaking Carlos Hathcock's record by 143.5 meters difference.

U.S. military sniper, Carlos Hathcock's record was in the Vietnam Civil War.

CHAPTER 13

THE SEMI-AUTOMATIC

"The semi-auto M1 Garand is the rifle that won World War 2."
—The Americans

I N 1898 JOHN BROWNING cracked the code on how to make a semi-automatic shotgun, meaning you only had to pull the trigger five times to get the five rounds off. When the round went off it would recoil the barrel a little, open the chamber, strip the dead casing out and two springs would raise a fresh round up then close the chamber. Browning called it the Auto-5.

When you're hunting ducks or geese you're shooting at multiple targets at once and that semi-auto system is a huge advantage over a double barrel break or a pump gun.

The Auto-5 ended John Browning's relationship with Winchester.

John Browning also used this concept in his 1911 handgun that was used by the U.S. Army from World War I to the Vietnam War. However it was replaced with the Berretta in the 1980's.

The first successful gas operated semi-automatic rifle was designed by a French Canadian working for the U.S. Army in 1932. His name was John Cantius Garand and his rifle was the M1 Garand. John Garand came up with a piston under the barrel. When the gun fired, the energy behind the bullet made the piston drive the chamber open and two springs inside the rifle would raise the next round up, the other would shut the chamber.

John Garand didn't just create the M1 Garand, he designed the machines that built his guns.

In 1936 the U.S. Army adopted the M1 Garand as their standard small arm. After the Japanese Air force bombed Pearl Harbor in

1941, Americas infantry soldiers were sent to Japan and Europe with M1 Garands in their arms.

Both the German and Japanese infantry were still using bolt-action rifles, meaning they had to grab a bolt, twist it, pull it back, push it forward and twist it again between shots, while an American with an M1 Garand just had to squeeze the trigger again and again for 8 rounds.

As good as the M1 Garand was, it had two flaws: it was semi-automatic only it can't be switched to fully-automatic and it can only be fired as fast it's operator could pull the trigger over and over. It's second flaw was that when it's last round was shot it made a very loud ping, telling your enemy that your rifle was empty.

The Americans did find a way to use the ping. The trick was to load your gun, keep an empty magazine (clip or magazine is the tube, box or belt attached to the gun that holds extra rounds) in your hand, shoot one round, throw the empty magazine on the ground. Making the same pinging sound, your enemy would react to the sound and stick his head up and then you'd get him.

The M1 Garand was used until the beginning of the Vietnam War.

The Americans will say that "the M1 Garand was the rifle that won World War II." However most Americans don't know that it came from the mind of one of Canada's greatest inverters, John Cantius Garand.

CHAPTER 14

THE MACHINE GUN

"It occurred to me that I could invent a machine, a gun that would by it's rapidity of fire, enable one man to do as much battle duty as a hundred."

—Dr. Richard Gatling

A LOT OF PEOPLE THINK of a machine gun as a weapon of mass destruction or a rapid firing killing machine. Very few people know that it was originally designed to save lives.

During America's Civil War, doctor Richard Gatling saw the heavy casualties that his men were taking.

He wondered how could he reduce the number of men on the battlefield. He wanted to come up with a gun that made one man do the job of a platoon of men with muzzleloaders. His answer was the Gatling gun.

It had six barrels, but was changed to ten that rotated as the operator cranked a handle that fired the gun continuously. As one barrel reloaded, one fired and one dropped a dead case, while the other 7 were cooling. On the test ground it worked but, in battle it's human operator made it a dead man's gun. When you have people shooting at you, your adrenalin became too high, you'd crank it too fast causing it to jam. This problem stopped it from being used long-term and it was eventually shelved. The Gatling gun eventually did came back in 1963, battery powered on the sides of military Blackhawk helicopters.

In the early 1880's American-born British Hiram Maxim was shooting his rifle. His gun's heavy kick was giving him pains in his shoulder and he was tired of chambering each shot. It was then he wondered, could he use one flaw to solve another. Can the recoil be used to chamber the next round?

In the mid 1880's he built a gun that fired 10 rounds a second and had a belt magazine. In 1889 the Maxim gun was put into service all the way up until the 1950's

In 1917 John Browning came up with his BAR or M1918 Browning Automatic Rifle. It was just a shade under 16 lbs but, it was tough and it was in service from 1918 to the beginning of the Vietnam War.

John Browning also came up with a great machine gun in 1918, the M2 Browning and it's still in used today.

The Maxim gun was good but, like all machine guns at the time it was heavy and you needed 3 people to move it on the battlefield, one man to carry the tripod, one to carry the ammo and a third to carry the gun itself. What was needed was a machine gun that an individual could carry, operate and fire alone. Three German brothers Fidel, Friedrich, and Josef Feederle were some of the first to come up with an answer with their Mauser C96 at the end of 1895, a handgun that had a full-auto capability.

In the Spanish American War an American Army officer named John T. Thompson also wanted a machine gun that one man could carry and sweep the trenches with. So he sat down at a drawing board and in 1920 he finished his trench broom "the Thompson submachine gun."

Unfortunate for John, by 1920 World War I was over and the American Army had no use for his gun, but someone else did. The Mafia, the IRA, the Al Capone gang and other gangsters all wanted something that sprayed bullets. In Chicago in those days it was illegal to walk around with a revolver in your pocket but there was no law stopping you from walking down the street with a Tommy gun in your arms. After gangsters got hold of this fire power, it forced the police to get Tommy guns of their own. The U.S. Army eventually adopted the Thompson and was used from World War II to the Vietnam War.

In the present day police departments have replaced the Tommy gun for the German made Heckler & Koch MP5.

CHAPTER 15
THE ASSAULT RIFLE

"I'm proud of my invention, but I'm sad that it is used by terrorists."
—Mikhail Kalashnikov

I N WORLD WAR II the Germans realized that there were combat situations that were too up-close for their Karabiner 98Ks and too far away for their MP 40s.

The Karabiner 98K is a bolt-action rifle that used the big 7.92×57mm Mauser bullet and it is accurate up to 1,000 meters. The MP 40 is fully-automatic and uses small pistol ammo. If you hit a human sized target over 50 meters with the MP 40 it was more luck than anything.

What was needed was a gun that could go on full-auto and that was reasonably accurate at long range. In 1943 the first assault rifle came on the battle field. The Sturmgewehr 44 used the Karabiner 98K's 7.92×57 round but, it was shrunken down from 57 down to 33mm making the gun controllable on full-auto.

The Sturmgewehr 44 was hidden from Hitler because the Germans thought that Hitler felt so passionate about the history he had, fighting in World War One with the 98k, he would reject the Sturmgewehr. Surprisingly when Hitler saw it's demonstration he was so impressed he called it the storm rifle.

The Sturmgewehr 44 came too late to save Germany from defeat, but it is the grandfather of the modern assault rifle, although other designs were not far behind it.

In the Soviet Union a sergeant tank commander named Mikhail Kalashnikov was seriously injured in 1944 fighting in World War II.

Before his injuries Mikhail Kalashnikov saw that almost all the German Waffen-SS had fully-automatic guns like the MP 18, MP 28, MP 40, MG 34 and MG 42 and that the SS did not save ammo. They shot anywhere they thought they could kill Russians. Mikhail set a goal to design something that could be mass produced quickly, was reliable and simple in order to compete with the SS. Mikhail Kalashnikov had designed guns before but, none were widely used.

This time was different. It was about defending his motherland from Nazi rule. As he was recovering in the hospital after his injuries he started working on his gun. The thing is that you don't design a gun overnight. It took him over two years to design. In 1947 he completed his creation and he called it the Avtomat Kalashnikova 1947. Everyone else called it the AK-47 but, by 1947 World War II was over and the Russians had no use for his gun.

In the U.S. after World War II the Americans knew they needed something to bridge the gap between the rifle and the submachine gun. There first answer was the M14.

The M14 was mainly an M1 Garand with a 20 round capacity and modified for fully-automatic fire. Unlike the submachine gun the M14 shot large bullets, the M14 used heavy 7.62×51 rounds but, it had problems. It and it's ammo were heavy, over 10 lbs when loaded and you could only carry about 150 rounds of ammunition. On fully-automatic fire its recoil made it spin out of control after 3 rounds. Your ammo is gone almost immediately with barely any hits but, at the time it was the Americans only practical option.

An American man named Eugene Stoner looked at the problems that the M14 had and figured he could solve them. He took a seat at the drawing board. Stoner knew in order to solve these problems the gun and bullet both had to be changed.

Stoner didn't just change it completely, he changed the materials. Stoner used fibreglass and plastic instead of wood. Only the barrel and a few moving parts were steel, all the other metal parts were aluminium. He threw away the heavy 7.62×51 bullet and replaced it with the much smaller 5.56×45. Stoner's assault rifle became the M16.

At first most Americans in the Army thought the M16 was a joke at the time because it's plastic parts and it's odd shape made it look like a toy.

In the early 1960's the AK-47 got it's chance on the battlefield in Vietnam. Large numbers of AK-47s were supplied to the North Vietnamese Army and some to the Viet Cong.

In the same war the U.S. Army decided to give the M16 a try. At first the American soldiers loved the M16, it was much lighter than the M14, it's small 5.56 meant you could carry twice as much ammo as opposed to what you would in a 7.62.

With Vietnam's dirty, rainy, muddy jungles and the ball powder in the ammo, the M16 started jamming in combat. There's no telling how many Americans died in Vietnam because their M16 jammed in battle. Eventually the ammo was changed to the cleaner stick powder and cleaning kits were given to the American troops. Army disciple made sure that soldiers cleaned their M16. You cleaned your gun before you brushed your teeth, you cleaned your gun before you got food, and you cleaned your gun before you cleaned yourself even though you might not have had a shower in a month. On the other side the less accurate AK-47 with it's looser fitting parts did not have this jamming problem. In fact, it was one of Mikhail Kalashnikov's driving points in the AK. Kalashnikov dragged his AK-47s through sand and after that they would fire without a hitch. The AK can be buried in sand, snow or mud and it will still work.

Even though the M16 was more accurate than the AK, in Vietnam it's accuracy didn't get much of a chance to shine. Most combat situations in Vietnam were in the thick jungles where you couldn't sometimes see more than 2-70 meters away and you're not trying to shoot an apple off someone's head. You're trying to hit a full-sized man that's less than 70 meters away so a more accurate gun was not going to guarantee an advantage in that kind of scenario.

In the end the North Vietnamese Army with their AKs and the Viet Cong booby traps defeated the Americans and South Vietnamese, winning the Vietnam War.

In the present-day the AK-47 and M16 designs are the two most widely used assault rifles in the world. In the Cold War the Russians would keep track of any country that would say they hated the United States and the Russians would practically give them AK-47s. So we've got AK-47s all over the world.

The AK-47 is very easy to use. You can give it to someone who never handled a gun before, give him or her 8 minutes of instructions and they can operate it. You can teach someone to take apart and clean an AK-47 in 3 hours. With an M16 you're going to need about six days.

The AK has made child soldiers more popular. (Child soldiers can be traced back to the 1770's in America's Revolutionary War where some fighters were as young as age 12.) In Cambodia's Civil War the average age of a Khmer Rouge guerrilla fighter was 16, some as young as 12 and in 1975 they defeated the Cambodian Army.

Today kids as young as age 7 use the AK-47 and when they're hopped up on cocaine, cannabis or brown-brown (brown-brown is smokeless gun powder mixed with cocaine) they're often more effective in combat than adults. The LRA use the AK-47 and most of those fighters are 7 to 15 years old. When it comes to child soldiers, their assault rifles, whether it's an AK-47, H&K G3, AK-74 or an M16, becomes a part of them and who they are. They sleep with them, they eat with them. It is with them 24/7 because it is their power, it is their life and if they don't use them they know that they will be killed. Ishmael Beah (the author of "A Long Way Gone") knows that better then most. He was a child soldier for two years, from age 13 to 15. He started out with an AK-47 and that gun kept him alive.

The AK-47 and M16 may be very different, however they did influence one another. The M16 originally had a 20-round magazine, the AK had a 30-round magazine. After the U.S. troops found this out they wanted a 30-round magazine for their M16s and they got them. In 1974 the M16's 5.56 that was lighter and tumbled in the body, was the inspiration for the AK-74 that used the smaller 5.45×39 as opposed to the AK-47's heavier 7.62×39.

In 1990 Mikhail Kalashnikov was invited to the U.S. to do an interview with Eugene Stoner. In this interview they explained their rifles to one another. Eugene explained to Mikhail that the U.S. Army demanded a very light system and that is why he used fibreglass in the M16. Mikhail reacted by saying that "all army people are the same. They all want weightless guns but, there is a limit to everything."

Eugene Stoner died seven years after the interview but, his M16 design is still being used by the U.S. and other armies around the world today.

Mikhail Kalashnikov died twenty-three years after the interview. His AK-47 is used by armies as well as terrorists, child soldiers, guerrilla fighters, Somali and other modern pirates as well as dictators like Osama bin Laden, Saddam Hussein and Joseph Kony. Mikhail Kalashnikov said, "It is frustrating to know that my gun is sometimes used by criminals but, how can we stop it, designers are not the ones to blame."

The M16 made Eugene Stoner into a millionaire. Mikhail Kalashnikov did not get rich off the AK because the communist system didn't allow that. He did become famous for inventing the most widely used assault rifle in the world.

The AK-47 has became an icon. Hezbollah and Mozambique put the AK-47 on their flags. Mozambique also put it on their coin.

In the 1980's Colt Canada created the C7 rifle. The C7 is an M16 like design with better reliability. It is in my opinion the best assault rifle in the world, like the M-16 it's light and accurate and like an AK-47 it's dependable. In the sandy conditions in Afghanistan they worked better than the M16 and from 2002 to 2011 the C7 in the hands of the Canadian Armed Forces gave the Taliban all they could handle.

The C7 is not just used by the Canadian Armed Forces and RCMP but, also by The Armed Forces of the Netherlands, the Norwegian Police, the Afghan National Army and three other forces in the United Kingdom.

Since the end of World War II the assault rifle has been used in almost every conflict around the world, from the C7 to the AK-47 to the M16, to the H&K G36 and the very widely used H&K G3.

May 2nd 2011: Almost ten years after the 9/11 attacks in New York, New York, United States, U.S. Navy SEAL Team 6 located Osama bin Laden in Abbottabad, Pakistan and shot him to death with the 5.56×45mm from the H&K 416 assault rifle. (a German gun based on the M16 platform) Osama bin Laden was hit twice, one to his chest the other right above his eye.

With the speed and weight of bullets like 5.56×45 and 5.45×39 they tumble over themselves when they hit something as dense as the human body instead of going straight through like bigger rounds. They are nasty, if one goes through your forearm not as big a deal. You might lose your hand but an ER doctor can keep you alive. When one hits almost anywhere else in the body it kills.

CHAPTER 16

WOMEN AND GUNS

"There is nothing sexier than a beautiful woman holding a good looking gun."
—Origin Unknown

GUN HATER ROSIE O'DONNELL is a woman. Most gun control supporters are women. Rebecca Peters was a spokesperson for IANSA, Rachel Maddow is an American news reporter, Wendy Cukier is a spokesperson for Canada's Coalition for Gun Control and Eleanor Holmes Norton led an anti-gun march in Washington D.C.

In the American sitcom "How I Met Your Mother," the Canadian character "Robin Scherbatsky" played by Canadian actress "Cobie Smulders" is a gun handler and enthusiast. I think the reason why the Americans find this funny is that most of them don't think of Canadians especially Canadian women as gun handlers.

I've noticed that a lot of people don't think of women as gun handlers but, history and modern day America tells me a very different story.

Joan of Arc was using a cannon in 1421 to defend France from British rule. She was one of the first women in history to use a firearm on a battlefield. Joan had no battlefield experience and evidence showing that she was dealing with schizophrenia. At only 17 years old Joan's intuition still allowed her to know exactly how to use this new kind of technology. As well as lead men into battle.

In Europe in the 15 and 1600's gun ownership was never restricted by gender, but by class. In 1600's England rich women carried small flintlock handguns on their person.

In the 1600's in Canada and the U.S. every house had a gun and every woman knew how to use theirs.

In America's Revolutionary War, Deborah Samson disguised herself as a man and joined the army with the fake name of Robert Shurtlieff. For three years none of her fellow recruits knew. She did suffer a slash injury to the neck and later a bullet wound to the thigh. She treated both injuries herself to make sure no one found out she was a woman and she dug the bullet out of her thigh with her knife. When she got brain fever she was discovered and had to apologize to General George Washington. George Washington was not just very forgiving, but gave her the money to cover her expenses to get home.

In the U.S.A.'s Civil War women fought in battle disguised as men on both sides using the same muzzleloaders and cannons as the men.

Today the U.S. and other armies around the world allow women to go into combat with the same firearms as their fellow male soldiers.

In Israel, military service is mandatory for it's citizens men and women.

Lots of women in the old west used guns for hunting. It was the old fashioned way of getting groceries.

Annie Oakley became one of the most famous sharp-shooters whether with rifle, shotgun or hand gun. She was good with them all.

Annie Oakley was extremely skilled with guns. She could shoot out a candle flame, and a dime out of someone's hands. At age 8 she was hunting and bagging animals to feed her family.

In her teens her hunting ability was so good she hunted commercially supplying birds for hotels. When Annie started shooting for show she always dressed very feminine. The reason for that was that she wanted to show that shooting guns is not just for men and that shooting guns is an either-sex sport, something that men and women should do together.

When she got older Annie became a teacher by teaching women how to shoot. Annie trained over 15,000 women in firearm usage for hunting, target shooting and self defence. Annie Oakley died on November 3rd 1926 at the age of 66.

Bonnie Parker and her boyfriend Clyde were outlaws. She was just as good with firearms as Clyde. Along with Clyde she made amazing escapes. She did pull guns on people but there is no evidence that she killed anyone. She and Clyde were ambushed and gunned down by Texas Rangers on a country road in May of 1934 when she was 23 years old.

We see women use guns on TV and in movies all the time. In the music video "Part Of Me" by Katy Perry she joins the U.S. Marine Corps. There she operates, carries and fires, from what I can tell looks like an M4 carbine.

Former Governor of the state of Alaska, Sarah Palin, is a hunter and gun rights supporter. Sarah Palin said that, "we eat, therefore we hunt."

American Sarah Merkle likes her AR-15. At 15 years old she started speaking out as a Gun Rights Supporter, a supporter of America's Second Amendment Right to The Constitution and goes by Wayne LaPierre's saying of, "the only way to stop a bad guy with a gun, is a good guy with a gun." Even if the good guy with a gun is not a guy.

Under the age of 20 American hunter Regis Giles created the website "GirlsJustWannaHaveGuns.com" to embrace other women to defend themselves with any means necessary, especially with guns.

In the 20th century women were beginning to be accepted in the military and trained with firearms. In Russia during World War II over 500,000 women were posted into regular army units. In the Vietnam Civil War some of the best Viet Cong fighters were women.

South of the border some American women carry their handguns in their purses, making them a rapist's worst nightmare. In 2005 13% of American women reported that they were gun owners and in 2011 it was up to 23%. Since 2012, female American gun ownership has been higher than ever before. Nearly 30,000,000 American women are gun owners today.

Just showing their guns stops 550 rapes and 1,100 murders every day in the United States.

The Smith & Wesson company makes guns specifically for women buyers, called the LadySmith.

Today in competitive shooting men and women compete on a level playing field. When a target is hit the gender of the shooter does not matter.

When it comes to the gun's recoil it's not as harsh on most women as it is on most men, because a lighter person is more pushed by the recoil. On a heavier person the gun's recoil hits harder because their weight holds them in place more and they don't go with the recoil as easily.

Since the mid 1970's the RCMP have had women on the force. They train with the same C7, Smith & Wesson 5946, H&K MP5 and Remington 870.

Sadly, because of Canada's gun laws and people with sexist attitudes, few women in this country are gun shooters today.

If you are a woman who would like to try shooting for any reason, you should not let Canada's harsh laws or sexism stop you. **Remember there is nothing unwomanly about shooting guns.**

If you have a fear of guns, just keep in mind that "when one of them is in your hands it is 100% under your control."

When it comes to guns, the cure for fear is knowledge.

First Time?

If you include airguns I started shooting firearms before I celebrated my fifth birthday and I have no memory of starting so I can't tell you what the first time is like. But I can tell you that when you hold them you feel secure and it feels like it's a part of you.

I recommend starting out with something in a .22 cal for a rifle or handgun. For a shotgun a .410 or a 20 gauge.

CHAPTER 17

ANTI-GUN VERSUS PRO-GUN

"Hate is more lasting than dislike."
—Adolf Hitler

"Gun control doesn't work."

"Gun control reduces violence."

"From my cold dead hands."
—Charlton Heston

"If you live by the gun, you die by the gun."

"Self defence is a human right."

"No Jews can have guns."
—Adolf Hitler

"The right of the people, To Keep And Bear Arms
shall not be infringed."
—America's 2nd Amendment

"Isn't one life worth it?"

"Banning Guns Only Hurts The People Who Mean
You No Harm."

"Guns kill people."

"Guns Don't Kill People, People Kill People."

"You are not allowed to own a gun, and if you do
own a gun I think you should go to prison"
—Rosie O'Donnell

"It's about freedom."

"It's about saving lives."

"Gun control has never saved anyone."

"The most foolish mistake we could possibly make
would be to allow the subject races to possess
arms. History shows that all conquerors who have
allowed their subject races to carry arms have

prepared their own downfall by so doing. Indeed, I would go so far as to say that the supply of arms to the underdogs is a sine qua non for the overthrow of any sovereignty."
—Adolf Hitler

"Any individual who acts in some way to try to stop people from protecting themselves. Any individual who would work to disarm people and often times that's known as gun control. The idea that a person should not have the tools to defend themselves. Anyone who is willing to be a part of that process of rendering the citizens defenceless is to blame."
—Richard W. Stevens

"You're as Bad as The Criminals"
"Anyone Who Wants To Disarm Me And Make Me Defenceless Can Drop Dead."
—Ted Nugent

"Guns should be banned."
"Suck On My Machine gun."
—Ted Nugent

"Weapons Designed For War Have No Place On Our Streets."
—Barack Obama

"Guns Don't Kill People, Guys With Pretty Daughters Kill People."

"Self Defence Puts Us All At Risk."

**"To disarm the people . . . was the best and most
effectual way to enslave them."**
—George Mason

"Call a Cop."

"An armed society is a polite society."
—Robert Heinlein

"Gun Play No Way."

**"Self-defence should be in your hands now, not
parked at Tim Hortons"**

"All We Ask Is Registration Just Like We do For Cars."
—Charles Shumer

**"Registration. Confiscation. GENOCIDE. Each
Step Makes The Next Step Much Easier."**

"The Owner is Gone . . . But The Gun Lives on."

**"Why do I carry a gun? Because a policeman is
too heavy."**

"Arms Are For Hugging."

"If guns cause crime, all mine are defective."
—Ted Nugent

"Protect The Children Not The Guns"

**"The Second Amendment of our Bill of Rights is
my Concealed Weapons Permit, period."**
—Ted Nugent

"Get Rid of the gun, it wouldn't have happened."

"Political Power Grows Out of the Barrel of a Gun."
—Chairman Mao

"Ban Guns Now and Stop Violence."
"Hitler. Stalin. Idi Amin. Pol Pot. The Experts
Agree Gun Control Works."
"Restricting access to firearms does not eliminate
gun violence, it reduces the risk."
—Wendy Cukier

"The only way to stop a bad guy with a gun, is a
good guy with a gun."
—Wayne LaPierre

"It's time for tough gun laws."
—Rebecca Peters

"Hitler, Stalin, Kony, Idi Amin, Pol Pot, Evil
prevails when gun control is established."
"Stop The NRA"
—IANSA

"If you take guns away from legal gun owners, then
the only people who have guns are the bad guys."
—Bruce Willis

"It is too easy to get a gun."
"It's preposterous that you can take a law, direct it
at the people who are already obeying the law, have

those same people obey more laws and expect to
have a different result."
—Tony Bernardo

> "1935 will go down in History! For the first time,
> a civilized nation has full gun registration! Our
> streets will be safer, our police more efficient and
> the world will follow our lead to the future!"
> —Adolf Hitler

SINCE THE TRAGEDY THAT occurred on December 14th, 2012 in Sandy Hook Elementary School in Newtown, Connecticut, United States, I'm sure you've probably heard some of or at least most of these sayings and quotes. I've heard them all so many times I can not remember where I heard most of them for the first time. These sayings and quotes all make a point and they are used by two enemies that will never find a way to coexist or find common ground. It is the Anti-gun people vs. the Pro gun people. People and criminals who are anti-gun want the law-abiding pro-gun people to get rid of their guns. Law-abiding people that are pro-gun refuse to back down and have had enough harassment from the anti-gun people. Like gay marriage and abortion there will never be laws on guns that will make both sides happy.

> "Make the lie big, make it simple, keep saying it, and eventually
> they will believe it."
> —Adolf Hitler

IANSA is short for **International Action Network on Small Arms.** Their office building is located in England and their main goal is to take the worlds guns away. Not from terrorists, not from the military, not from the LRA and not from the RCMP but from Olympic shooters, hunters and other law-abiding honest people.

Even over 200 years after the American Revolutionary War IANSA is still labelling the NRA (National Rifle Association), the NFA (National Firearms Association), 89% of Americans and 30.8% of Canadians as evil. IANSA wants to destroy the American's 2nd Amendment along with the NRA and the NFA. They are very persuasive and good at spreading their poison about law-abiding people. Like the KKK and the Nazis, IANSA use brainwashing and propaganda to make people think in the negative way that, "self defence is dangerous to everyone and that it is better to be a victim of rape or murder than to have the right to protect yourself."

IANSA funding comes from billionaire gun-hater George Soros, donations and even from UNICEF.

Most people don't know that UNICEF is a partner with IANSA. The kids that showed up on your doorstep back in the 90's on Halloween with UNICEF boxes, were helping IANSA ban your guns if you are a gun owner.

With UNICEF, IANSA uses sick and dying kids to get funding to take away your right to protect yourself. They use violence to ban what really is a human right. Personally they make me sick for using children like that.

In the 1990's IANSA banned handguns with shorter than 4.1 inch barrels. In Canada that was over 58% of them registered since 1935.

Canada's Coalition For Gun Control claim that they're making this country a safer place but, when you're unarmed and a killer has a black market weapon, they are really protecting the violent criminals that may want to kill and/or rape you.

IANSA, the Million Mom March and Canada's Coalition For Gun Control all want the same thing the criminals want: you defenceless.

If it wasn't for the U.S., the NFA and the NRA, IANSA and Canada's Coalition For Gun Control would have taken everything away a long time ago.

The NRA was formed November 17th 1871 to protect Americas freedom and it's 2nd Amendment. They also have a seat at the UN.

The NRA's goal is to stop the criminals by fear. What criminals fear most is not prison or the police but you, a law-abiding person <u>who might be armed</u> that will pull a gun out to save their own life.

Put yourself in a criminals shoes, which victim would you pick between, an unarmed one or one that might have a gun who will fight back?

The NRA also wants to arm law-abiding women. Why?

When a 180 lb homicidal junkie who's hopped up on PCP or Crystal Meth breaks into the house of a 110 lb woman who lives alone or has small children, the psycho will win that fight every time but, when you put an AR-15 in that woman's hands with 30-rounds of rock "n" roll in it, the tables are 100% turned.

Guns in the hands of the law-abiding citizens in the U.S. stop criminals countless times a year. You never hear about it because, who reports a crime that **does not** happen? The estimate is that firearms are used to stop crime five time more often then they are used to commit them.

The law-abiding Americans in Alabama, Alaska, Arizona, Arkansas, the two Carolinas, Colorado, Connecticut, both Dakotas, Florida, Georgia, Indiana, Iowa, Kansas, Kentucky, Louisiana, Maine, Michigan, Minnesota, Mississippi, Missouri, Montana, Nebraska, Nevada, New Hampshire, New Mexico, Ohio, Oklahoma, Oregon, Pennsylvania, Taxes, Tennessee, both Virginias, Vermont, Washington and Wyoming can get Right to Carry permits.

As a Canadian who has grown up with strict gun laws and a long gun registry from 1995 to 2012, I can see why we might find it strange that a law-abiding civilian can legally carry a sidearm almost anywhere in these States.

The NFA, like the NRA in the U.S., strongly supports the promotion of rights of marksmanship, firearm safety and the protection of hunting and self-defence, but the NRA and NFA oath stops them from ever being the aggressor.

The NFA is Canada's NRA. If it weren't for the NFA, IANSA would have made semi-automatics and handguns illegal in Canada.

- In 1997 IANSA completely banned handguns in England. After the ban violent gun crime went up by 49%. For the first time in England criminals are carrying guns, the police had to trade their clubs in for guns and there are over 300,000 illegal guns on England's streets. For the population, England's violent crime rate is now 3.5 times higher than the U.S. thanks in part to IANSA.

- IANSA banned semi-automatic and pump guns in Australia. Since then gun murders went up 19%, home invasions went up 21%, assault with guns went up 28% and armed robberies went up 69%.

- In July of 2004 IANSA established harsh gun control in South Africa. Since the ban there have been 15 murders every month on farms alone. Since 1994 over 13,000 police officers have been killed for their guns, law-abiding women raped at gun point by criminals. The police are outgunned by the criminals of South Africa who steal firepower from the police, smuggle guns over the borders of Namibia, Botswana, Zimbabwe, Mozambique and Swaziland and buy AK-47's and H&K G3's off the black market. Africa is already so flooded with AK-47's and AK-74's, that in some parts of the continent you can trade a bag of food for one. Having South Africa's law-abiding civilians unarmed, the criminals are taking their toll.

Australia, South Africa and England have become living proof of John R. Lott, Jr.'s saying of, "more guns, less crime." You can't help but wonder that if Australia, South Africa and England had an association like the NFA or an organization like the NRA, they would probably still be reasonably safe.

Commander of the 3rd Reich Adolf Hitler and Cambodian Dictator Pol Pot might be dead and no longer lead the Nazis or the Khmer Rouge but, Wendy Cukier and George Soros are both very much alive.

Wendy Cukier still leads Canada's Coalition For Gun Control.

George Soros still funds IANSA.

Gun control has been used to torture and kill millions of people all over the world in the past 150 years. This might make people wonder, what goes on inside the mind of a Gun Control Activist? There are actually three answers to that question.

1. Some have been convinced by IANSA and other anti-gun organizations like Canada's Coalition For Gun Control that guns are bad in the hands of the law-abiding.
2. Most commonly, gun control gives these people a false sense of protection.
3. They think everybody is dangerous with a gun.

Canada's Coalition For Gun Control and IANSA will say that gun control keeps people safe. But when you look at Mexico and Uganda where it is illegal for civilians to have guns, you are way more likely to die from gunshot wounds there than in the United States which has one of the lowest gun control laws in the world.

In Mexico it is illegal for non police and non military to own guns and in 2011 alone over 20,000 civilians and policeman there died from gunshot injuries from the Mexican Drug Cartel.

What Canada's Coalition For Gun Control won't tell you is that today in the United States, where 89% of the citizens are gun owners, guns are used in self-defence approximately two million times a year (five times more than are used to commit crime) by law abiding American citizens.

57% of American felons are more terrified by armed victims than the American police.

Even with 11,000 gun shot deaths a year in the U.S. over 90% of them are suicide and Japan has double the suicide rate with a smaller population and very harsh gun laws. Another thing that Canada's Coalition For Gun Control and IANSA will not admit or tell you is that . . .

- In 1928, Germany established gun registration and in 1938 Adolf Hitler used it to established gun confiscation. From 1939 to 1945, over **20,000,000** unarmed innocent Jews and others who were unable to defend themselves were rounded up, tortured and executed.
- In 1917, the Soviet Union established gun control. From 1929 to 1953, over **20,000,000** unarmed innocent people, unable to defend themselves were rounded up, tortured and executed.
- In 1911, Turkey established gun control. From 1915 to 1917, **1,500,000** unarmed innocent Armenians, unable to defend themselves were rounded up, tortured and executed.
- In 1935, China established gun control. From 1942 to 1952, **35,000,000 to 100,000,000** unarmed innocent political

dissidents, pro-reformists and Chinese civilians unable to defend themselves were rounded up, tortured and executed.

- In 1964, Guatemala established gun control. From 1964 to 1981, **1,500,000** unarmed innocent Mayan Indians, unable to defend themselves were rounded up, tortured and executed.

- In 1956 Cambodia, King Sihanouk established harsh gun control and in 1975 Pol Pot established gun confiscation. From 1975 to 1979, over **2,000,000** innocent foreign and educated people, unable to defend themselves were rounded up, tortured and executed.

- In 1994, Rwanda established gun control. Since then over **800,000** unarmed innocent people were unable to defend themselves, have been rounded up, tortured and executed so far.

- In 1970 Uganda, Milton Obote established gun control. From 1970 to the present-day, over **702,400** unarmed innocent people, unable to defend themselves have been rounded up, raped, tortured, executed, and that number is still on the rise.

- In the 1870's the United States established gun control. From the 1870's to 1968, **10,000's** of unarmed innocent African Americans, unable to defend themselves were beaten and murdered.

- In 1995, Canada established gun control. From 1995 to the present-day, **1,000's** of unarmed innocent people unable to defend themselves, were raped and/or murdered.

Whoever said, "the pen is mightier than the sword," clearly was not a Jewish German Holocaust survivor. Whoever said, "gun control reduces crime and violence," clearly was not a Ugandan LRA survivor and was very out of touch with reality.

From 1619 to the present-day over **170,000,000** defenceless innocent people have been raped, tortured, used as slaves and executed around the world because of gun control. To me that is not peace or war, that is madness.

Adolf Hitler, Joseph Stalin, Pol Pot, Idi Amin and Joseph Kony are very sick evil people but, in a strange way fascinating because they're leaders and of what they were/are able to get other human beings to do and **they all used gun control to massacre millions of innocent unarmed people, men, women, children, and babies.** They're evil and we should hate giving evil people this much attention but, if we don't recognize these evil leaders and call them for what they are, they will brainwash people, feed them propaganda and establish gun control costing more innocent people their lives.

Suzanna Gratia, the teachers of Dawson College, Columbine, Virginia Tech, Sandy Hook and the people that are LRA, genocide and holocaust survivors live with something extremely horrible, that anti-gun people do not understand. These survivors have emotional scars and nightmares. Every day they play in their heads over and over, "I wish I was warned, I wish I could have done something about this, I wish I had a gun, I wish I could have fought back. I wish I could have saved my children, family, my fellow teachers and my students." That pain of mind never goes away for them.

Gun rights have always been and will always be the difference between freedom and oppression. When innocent people accept gun control and being unarmed, the guilty rape them, or kill them with any weapon they wish, a knife, a bat, broken glass or a plastic bag.

A large number of people have the ability to kill smaller weaker people with their own hands (with one of the ways pioneered by Alexander the Great.) It only takes 70 pounds of pressure to crush the human trachea and cause death so for a lot of us our feet and elbows are weapons that can kill.

What can you do when self-defence is illegal and you're attacked by a mad man? Or when your own Government betrays you and wants you dead because of your religion, your skin colour, what you know, your sexuality or just for being who you are?

That's how it was for the Vietnamese, Chinese and educated people of Cambodia.

That's how it was for the people of Guatemala.

That's how it was for the people of China.

That's how it was for the Armenian people of Turkey.

That's how it was for the people of Russia.

That's how it was for the Jewish, Gypsy, handicapped and homosexual people of Germany.

That's how it was for the African Americans of the United States.

That's how it is for the people of Uganda.

That's how it is for the people of Mexico.

That's how it is for the people of Rwanda.

They say, "Evil prevails when good men fail to act." I say, "Evil prevails when gun control is established." Uganda, Australia, England, South Africa, Turkey, China, Guatemala, Russia, The U.S., Germany, Cambodia and Rwanda are living proof of that.

If harsher gun control laws made people safer, then Uganda and Mexico would be the safest places on earth, and the United States would be the most dangerous place on earth. And it is very clear that it is the other way around.

The Mexican Drug Cartel and the Lord's Resistance Army both use the combination of gun control and black market weapons to out-gun the Police & Armies of their countries, and kill tens of thousands of the innocent law-abiding civilians every year.

After Sandy Hook the anti-gun people keep calling the AR-15 an assault rifle and it is not. The AR-15 can only fire one round every time it's trigger is pulled and can only fire as fast as it's human operator can squeeze it's trigger. It is not all that different from your standard semi-auto hunting rifle. What really bothers the anti-gun people is that the AR-15 **LOOKS** a lot like it's old brother, the M16 which can go on fully-automatic and is an assault rifle.

The AR-15 and M16 are similar <u>in appearance</u> and have a similar gas system but the main difference is that an M16 can switch from semi-automatic to fully-automatic. Your standard AR-15 can not do this. To get an AR-15 to go on full-auto you have to take it apart, obtain certain parts, assemble those parts into the gun yourself and put the gun back together. Anti-gun people automatically assume a gun is more dangerous just because it has a plastic stock, looks modern or has a pistol grip as strange as that sounds.

Robert Heinlein said that, "An armed society is a polite society." I believe that there is a lot of truth to that.

In America self-defence is legal and in America the criminals fear the law-abiding. In Canada it is the other way around.

The gun control debate is on! Not just in politics but in organizations.

The National Firearms Association	**International Action Network on Small Arms**
The National Rifle Association of America	**Canada's Coalition For Gun Control**
The Canadian Shooting Sports Association	**The Ku Klux Klan**
LRA Survivors	**The Million Mom March**

THE NAMES BEHIND GUN CONTROL

Joseph Stalin, Andrew Cuomo, Adolf Hitler, David Raymond Miller, Chairman Mao, Pol Pot, Rachel Maddow, Idi Amin, George Soros, Rebecca Peters, Michael Bloomberg, Barack Obama, Wendy

Cukier, Eleanor Holmes Norton, Bill Maher, Rosie O'Donnell, Jean Chrétien, Michael Ignatieff and Dylan Klebold.

> "It is not truth that matters, but victory."
> —Adolf Hitler

> "I have built my organization upon fear."
> —Al Capone

Anti-gun groups today use the internet to promote their fears, lies and propaganda.

Propaganda lying worked better before the internet. With TV or radio they could put out a certain message to a large number of people and bend those people to their will. With the present-day internet, propaganda is a very difficult thing to do because you have freedom of speech combined with the fact that everyone has access to it.

> "The truth is found when men are free to pursue it."
> —Franklin D. Roosevelt

There are anti-gun governments that do have people who monitor what others are doing on the internet. Having said that, today there are more people on facebook alone than there were people on the entire planet during The War of 1812. So no government not Canada, North Korea, the U.S. or even China can control the amount of information that is being exchanged.

In a debate of any kind the truth is the most powerful weapon that can be used. The truth about what gun control really does to people, the lies that anti-gun groups have told people are now exposed and are spreading across the internet.

We cannot ignore gun control for the same reason we can not ignore cancer or racism. If we ignore cancer and the KKK they're not going to go away. If we ignore gun control it's not going to go away.

Anti-gun people have asked: "Why do you want a handgun or a machine gun?" Here are the answers.

1. Collection.
2. They're fun to shoot.
3. Self defence.
4. The human instinct of wanting what we are not allowed to have.

I would like to set the tone straight that with this book I am **NOT celebrating** the Nazi party, the Khmer Rouge, the Ku Klux Klan, the International Action Network on Small Arms, Canada's Coalition For Gun Control, The Million Mom March, James Roszko, Wendy Cukier, Kimveer Gill, George Hennard, Eric Harris, Dylan Klebold, Seung-Hui Cho, Adam Lanza, Rosie O'Donnell, George Soros, Rebecca Peters, Eleanor Holmes Norton, Joseph Stalin, Michael Bloomberg, David Raymond Miller, Andrew Cuomo, Rachel Maddow, Bill Maher, Adolf Hitler, Idi Amin, Pol Pot or Joseph Kony at all.

They're dangerous but, if we don't know who the dangerous people are and what they are up to, we won't know how to stop them before they cause horrible levels of violence.

Some things, like the right of self-defence, are worth fighting for.

The information of this book was obtained from:

Global: Original Documentary Revealed Missing the Target

CTV News

NRA documents

ATF

FBI

The Smith & Wesson company

IANSA

Canada's Coalition For Gun Control

Eugene Stoner

Mikhail Kalashnikov

Wayne LaPierre

Suzanna Gratia

Jesse Ventura

Scott Paddor

Silvio Wolf Busch (Former German Military)

Robert Wilhelm-McCain (German Military Historian)

Jason Heck (16th Century Weapons Expert)

Jim Dunham (Historian)

Llewellyn M. Smith

Fernando Vazquez

Timothy Pickles (Military Historian)

Ishmael Beah (Former Child Soldier)

Frank Cook (Member of British Parliament)

? (British Police Officer who asked to remain anomies)

? (Australian Police Officer who asked to remain anomies)

? (South African Police Officer who asked to remain anomies)

Wolfgang Pollman (Saskatoon Police)

Philip Schreier

Joey Dillon

Nate Thayer

Ann Coulter

Richard W. Stevens

Aaron Zelman

Piers Morgan

Ginny Simone

Michael Moore

John Stossel

WNWO News

Firearm Safety class the documentary of AK-47 the documentary of
The Life of Pol Pot the documentaries of Declassified the documentaries
from The Most Evil Men in History times and dates from an information
internet website known as www.wikipedia.org

Greatest Military Clashes M16 v AK-47

The Canadian Armed Forces the documentaries from Deadliest Warrior

Fox News

Bureau of Justice Statistics

National Institute of Justice

KONY 2012

KONY 2012: Part II Beyond Famous

Several other reliable references that will remain anonymous.

www.ingramcontent.com/pod-product-compliance
Lightning Source LLC
Chambersburg PA
CBHW050356290526
45786CB00003B/1017